BIBLE
BIRDS AND
BEASTIES

Contents

Creatures Great and Small

In the beginning, God made the whole world. God made light to shine in the darkness; dry ground in the middle of salty seas; and planets and stars, the sun and moon, day and night.

And God made creatures in the sea, on the land, and in the sky: scaly fish and snapping crocodiles; feathered flamingos and proud peacocks; leaping lizards, terrifying tigers, and raging rhinos; calm cows, plump pigs, and creepy crawlies; chattering chimps, silent sloths, zigzag zebras, and long-necked giraffes.

Many shapes and different sizes, funny smells and snorty noises—God made all creatures, big ones and little ones.

But God wanted a creature who would share His likeness, a creature who could love and be loved, think and feel and create; a creature who was capable of caring about others and who would look after His world. So God made man and woman.

God looked at all that He had made, and it was very good.

Lots of Birds and Beasties

God was angry about sin in the world, so He decided to wash away all the earth. God told Noah it was going to rain very, very hard. Soon there would be a great flood. Everything would be washed away—except Noah, his family, and all kinds of birds and beasties.

God told Noah to build an ark—a huge boat—and to fill it with lots of food. Then Noah should wait for the rain to come.

When the ark was ready, the animals came down from the trees and across the land. They padded, plodded, galloped, hopped, jumped, scampered, slithered, and crawled in through the door.

Two by two, male and female, the animals crowded into the ark. It was hot. It was noisy. It was SMELLY!

Noah and his family climbed aboard and BANG! God shut the door.

A Raven, a Dove, and a Rainbow

Splish, splash, splish, splash, the rain began to fall.

Steadily, heavily, the rain fell on the streams until they became rivers, the rivers became seas, and the seas covered the earth and the trees and the mountains . . . until there was nothing left to see, except the ark, floating on the water.

After forty days and forty nights, God made the rain stop. Noah and his family and the animals listened. There was nothing, no sound at all.

Then days and weeks and months passed. Slowly, slowly, the floodwaters went down. The sun came out, and slowly, slowly, the land dried up.

Noah set free a raven and then a dove. Both birds came back to the ark. Noah set free a second dove until . . . flap, flap, coo, coo, it returned carrying an olive leaf in its beak.

Finally, God told Noah it was safe for his family and the animals to come out of the ark.

The animals hooted and tooted, roared and bleated and trumpeted as they spread out from the ark on to the new, clean earth.

Then God sent a beautiful rainbow.

"There will never be a flood like this again," God promised. And God keeps His promises!

Noah thanked God for keeping them safe from the flood.

The Patient Camels

The camels sneezed as the dust swirled all around them. It was time to set off again across the rough, stony ground. They were off to Egypt.

Young Joseph's hands were tied together and fastened to a rope. All he could see in front of him as he stumbled through the sand were the backs of the patient camels.

"Where are we going?" he cried desperately. No one answered. The only sound was the soft padding of the camels' hooves.

Joseph knew he was in big trouble. It had all started with the coat his father had given him—a fantastic coat of many colors!

But it made his older brothers so jealous that they planned to get rid of him. First, they threw him into a deep well. Then, they pulled him out of the well and sold him, their own brother, to these traders who were going to faraway Egypt!

But God had great plans for Joseph in Egypt. When he grew up, Joseph would be second only to the great king in wealth and power. And one day, Joseph would save his whole family from starvation.

But this was a future Joseph could not even imagine as he stumbled in the sand behind the patient, plodding camels.

Beasties in Egypt

Moses, and all God's people, had been made slaves by the cruel ruler of Egypt. Now, Moses stood in front of Pharaoh himself, with a message that sounded so bold it was frightening.

"God says that you must set His people free, or there will be trouble you cannot even imagine," Moses said.

The king would not listen. So God sent terrible plagues on the land of Egypt.

The river turned to blood. The land was covered with thousands of frogs that found their way into beds and cooking pots!

There were plagues of biting gnats and buzzing flies. Then the cows, sheep, goats, and horses fell ill and died. There were painful sores on the skin of all the Egyptians. Hail rained down on the land, smashing the crops in the fields. A plague of locusts came to eat up anything left after the hailstorm. Darkness covered the land. And then, the most terrible plague of all—all the Egyptian firstborn sons, including Pharaoh's own son, died in a single night.

"God says, 'Let My people go!'" said Moses to Pharaoh.

"Yes!" said Pharaoh in despair. "Go!"

Moses did not wait for Pharaoh to change his mind! He led God's people out of Egypt, the land where they had been slaves. He led them on their journey to the Promised Land, where they would be free.

The Donkey That Saw an Angel

Balaam thought he was smarter than God.
One day, Balaam set off on a journey with his
donkey—even though God had told him not to go.

As they started out, an angel appeared, holding
a sword and blocking their path!

The donkey saw the angel and turned off the
road into a field. But Balaam was not as wise as the
donkey. He did not see the angel. He beat the poor
old donkey with a stick. Ouch!

The donkey got back on the road. But now, the angel was standing in a narrow path between two walls. The donkey jumped to one side and squashed Balaam's leg against the wall.

Still, Balaam did not see the angel! He couldn't understand why the donkey was being so awkward. He beat her again with his stick. Ouch!

The angel moved on ahead of them to a place where there was no room to turn around. The donkey could do nothing else but stop and lie on the ground.

Balaam's Talking Donkey

Balaam beat his donkey with his stick. He was very angry.

But since Balaam was not wise enough to see the angel, God made the donkey speak to him.

"What have I done to you? Why have you hit me three times with your stick?" cried the donkey.

Balaam was astounded. "You've made me look foolish!" he answered.

"But I'm your dear old donkey!" said the animal.

18

"I have never disobeyed you before. Surely you knew I wouldn't do it now without good reason!"

Then Balaam saw the angel too.

"Why have you beaten your donkey three times?" asked the angel. "She saved your life by turning away and not trying to pass me."

"I was stubborn," Balaam answered. "I should have listened to God and done what He told me. I am sorry! I will do whatever He asks!"

The donkey never spoke again, but Balaam was careful to listen—to God!

The Donkeys That Wandered

God's people wanted to have a king so they could be like the countries around them. Who should be their king? they wondered.

God told the prophet Samuel that Saul would come to him, looking for his father's lost donkeys.

Saul was a tall, handsome young man. When the donkeys wandered off, Saul took a servant and looked everywhere for them.

"We could ask Samuel, the man of God," said the servant. "If anyone knows, he will."

When Samuel saw Saul coming toward him, God told him that this was the man who would be king.

"I know what you are looking for," Samuel said to Saul. "But don't worry about the missing donkeys. They are safe. But I am looking for you! Come with me."

After they had eaten together, Samuel poured some oil over Saul's head. "God has a special job for you to do," he said, "and God will help you do it well."

Saul found the wandering donkeys—and he found much more at the same time. Now he knew what God wanted him to do with his life. He would be the first king of Israel.

The Helpful Ravens

Elijah had made himself very unpopular with wicked King Ahab.

He had given the king a special message from God—if Ahab did not stop worshiping statues made of wood and stone, then God would not send rain to the earth. Ahab was so angry about this message that Elijah feared for his life and ran away!

No rain fell on the earth. Weeks passed, and the earth became dry and cracked. The rivers dried up. But faithful Elijah knew that God would look after him.

God told Elijah where to hide from the angry king. "Drink from the water of this stream," said God, "and I will send ravens with food for you."

God kept His promise.

When Elijah was thirsty, he drank the clear water from
the stream. When he was hungry, he waited for the ravens to
come. There would be a flapping of black wings, and the large
black birds appeared. Every morning and evening they brought
meat and bread to Elijah. God gave him everything he needed.

The ravens kept coming until God said it was time for Elijah
to move on.

A Big Fish and a Stormy Sea

Jonah was sinking deep into the salty sea in the middle of a terrible storm. He was sure he would drown. And he knew it was all his fault.

You see, Jonah had tried to run away from God. He was supposed to go to the city of Nineveh to tell the people there to stop doing bad things. He was supposed to tell them that God would forgive them if they would change their ways. But Jonah didn't want to go to Nineveh. It was a scary place. Jonah thought the wicked people who lived there deserved God's punishment!

So Jonah ran away from God. He jumped aboard a ship sailing the other way. But when a terrible storm came, Jonah knew God had caused the storm to stop him from running away. Jonah told the sailors to throw him into the choppy waves.

The Fish That Swallowed a Man

Now all Jonah could do was pray. He called out to God—and God saved him.

God sent a huge fish to swallow Jonah. The fish opened its mouth, and in went Jonah. He lived in the body of the fish for three days. It was very dark, and it smelled very fishy.

But Jonah had time to think and to pray.

He was sorry he hadn't done what God had asked him to do. He knew that if he got out of the fish, he had to go to Nineveh.

The big fish spat Jonah out on to the beach.

The next time God spoke, Jonah listened. He went to the people of Nineveh and gave them God's message. And the people listened. They stopped doing wicked things and asked God to forgive them. And because God loved them, He did.

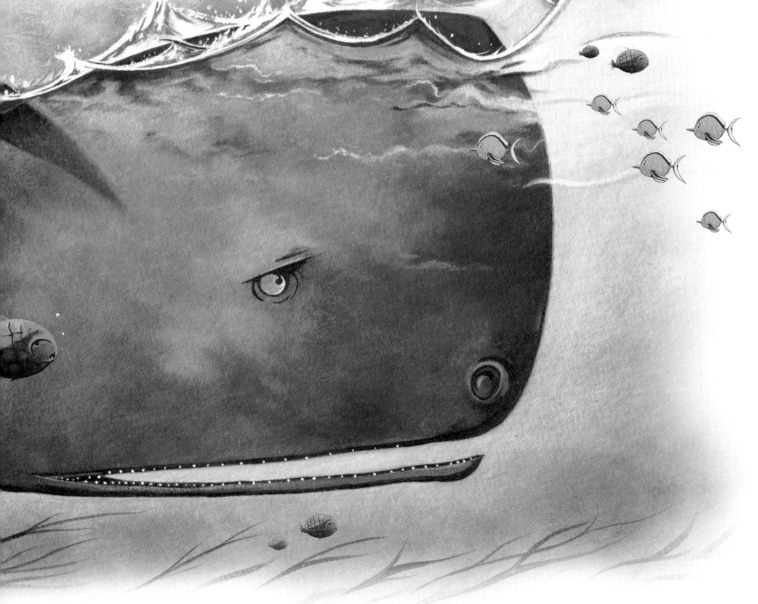

The Tight-Mouthed Lions

Daniel loved God. So when a law was made in Babylon that everyone must pray only to the king, Daniel could not obey it. He prayed to God alone because he was faithful to God.

It was no surprise when Daniel was tied up and dragged away to be thrown into a den of hungry lions. He had broken the law. But the lions went hungry that night. God sent an angel to close their mouths so that Daniel, God's faithful servant, would be safe.

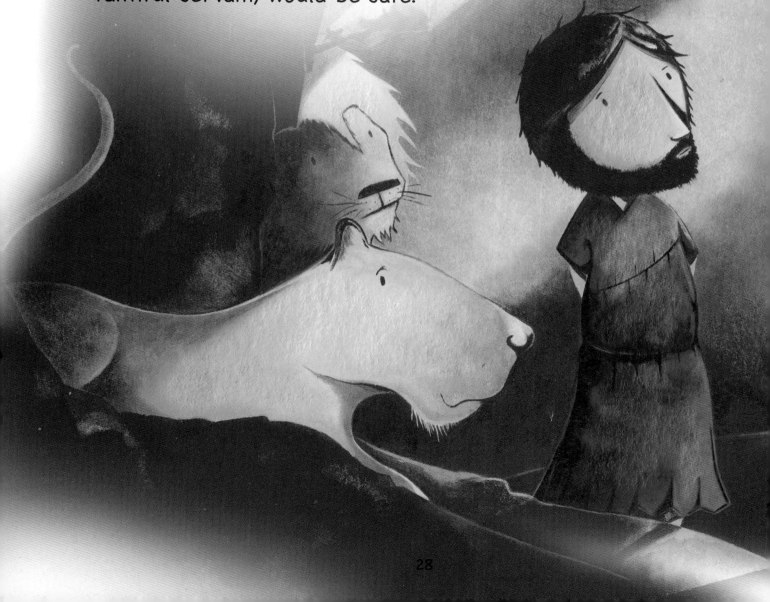

Night came and went. The king, who had been tricked into passing the law by Daniel's enemies, hurried to the den at first light.

"Daniel! Daniel! Has your God saved you?" the king shouted.

"Yes!" called out the man among the lions. "God saved me from the lions. God knows that I love Him and did nothing wrong."

The king was overjoyed. He commanded the soldiers to release Daniel.

"Now everyone in the land will worship the God of Daniel," said the king, "for He has the power to save us, even from the mouths of lions."

A Baby in the Cattle Shed

Outside was the sound of the crickets. Inside was the sound of calves snuffling in the straw and the ox and donkey munching on the hay.

Mary tried to rest. This was not how she imagined the birth of her firstborn Child would be. She thought she would be at home, with her mother and neighbors to help her. She thought she would be lying in her own bed in Nazareth. But she was here in Bethlehem, surrounded by animals, with only Joseph, her husband, to help.

But Mary remembered the words of the angel Gabriel, who had told her she would be the mother of God's own Son: "Do not be afraid, Mary."

The cry of an infant broke the stillness of the night, and Mary cradled her new baby in her arms.

"Hello, baby Jesus," she whispered. She wrapped her Son in clean cloths and held Him close. Then she put Him in the manger to sleep, while the animals looked on.

The Sheep That Heard Angels

The sheep were sleeping on the hills near Bethlehem. Some were cuddled together; some were still bleating as they tried to get comfortable for the night.

Suddenly, the sky was filled with dazzling light! The sheep and the shepherds woke up. They all stared at the sight of first one, then many angels filling the sky.

"Don't be afraid!" the angel of the Lord said. "I have come to bring good news! A baby has been born today who is the Savior of the world, Christ the Lord. Go to Bethlehem, where you will find Him wrapped in cloths and lying in a manger."

What could this mean? Angels, here, visiting ordinary shepherds with their sheep? Then the sound of angels singing filled the air:

"Glory to God in the highest, and on earth, peace to everyone. To you this day is born a Savior!"

There had never been such a wonderful sight; it was the glory of heaven. There had never been such a beautiful sound; it was the music of heaven.

There had never been such wonderful news; He was Christ the Lord!

Then, the shepherds left their sheep and went to find the special baby.

The Camels That Followed a Star

The camels knelt as their masters placed brightly colored rugs over them. The men secured their packs and climbed into the saddles. The camels rose, back legs first, to their feet and turned their heads to the tug of the harnesses.

The dark night was studded with stars. One seemed brighter and larger—a jewel among all the others. The camels saw that this star was always before them on the journey. The camels and their masters were following this bright star.

"A new star," said one of the men, seated high on the camel's back. "A sign in the heavens; the birth of the Child born to be King of the world."

"How long do you think it will take us to find Him?" asked another, bouncing along in his saddle.

"A long time," said the other. "But we'll find Him. The star will guide us to the right place."

Camels, Gifts, and a King

The camels were pleased to stop in Jerusalem. The streets were narrow, and the houses were built close together, but there was food and water, even for camels.

Their rest was short. The king here did not look happy that they were there. But he waved good-bye to them and sent them on their way along the cobbled streets and back on the sandy road, with the bright star still shining in front of them.

The house where they stopped was on hilly ground, but there was a warm light inside. A woman stood with a young child in her arms.

"We have come to worship the new King!" said one of the men. "We have traveled from the East."

The men opened their packs and presented the beautiful gifts they had brought with them: gold, frankincense, and myrrh, gifts for a King. Then they bowed low to worship her Son, whose name was Jesus, before returning home.

Mary treasured their gifts, but she sat thoughtfully, wondering at the words of these men who had traveled so far to see the baby Jesus.

The Little Sparrows

There were many amazing creatures among those God made.

Some had long necks and some had funny tails. Some had pretty feathers and some had scaly skins. Some had stripes and some had spots.

Sparrows fluttered about in hundreds. The little brown birds were not the largest or the most beautiful of God's creatures. But God loved each one of them.

When Jesus grew up, He told people many things about God. He told them that loving God and following His ways would be the best thing they ever did. But it would not be easy.

Jesus told them that some people would be unkind to them. Sometimes doing the right thing would be difficult. But Jesus told people not to be afraid. He pointed to the little brown birds hopping around them.

"Two sparrows are sold for a penny," said Jesus. "But God feeds them and looks after them. He knows when they fly from their nests, and He knows when they fall. If God cares about the sparrows, then you can be sure that He cares even more about you! He knows everything—even how many hairs are on your head. So don't be afraid. God promises to take care of you."

The Very Special Sheep

Jesus often told stories to explain what God was like. Once He told this story about a shepherd who owned a hundred sheep:

"The sheep were all shapes and sizes, young and old, fat and scrawny. But they had one thing in common. They were all special to the shepherd. He loved each one of them and cared for them, night and day. He made sure they had food and water, and he protected them from danger."

Jesus said, "Wolves and bears crept about at night, trying to snatch the lambs away from the flock. But the shepherd had a strong stick to protect his sheep. He didn't want even one of them to be taken by wild animals or thieves."

A Lost Sheep Is Found

"One day, a shepherd counted his sheep and noticed that he had only ninety-nine. One sheep was missing.

"The shepherd set off to find his lost sheep. He looked over the high ground, in the valleys, behind rocks, inside caves. The shepherd called out in a loud voice.

"Then he heard a faint bleating sound. The lost sheep had heard his voice and recognized him.

"The shepherd untangled the sheep from the thorns,
lifted him up onto his shoulders, and carried him home.
" 'Look!' the shepherd called to his friends. 'I've
found my lost sheep! What a happy day it is for me!' "
Jesus is sometimes called the Good Shepherd.
He cares about all of His little ones, just
like the shepherd in the story He told.

The Colt That Carried a King

Princes and kings choose the finest horses to ride. They sit high up in the saddle, and everyone knows they are important. Even *they* think they are important.

But when Jesus, the King of kings, rode into Jerusalem, He didn't choose a fine horse. Jesus chose a gentle, ordinary colt.

The colt had been standing with its mother when two men came and untied them. They placed blankets over the colt's back and helped Jesus climb on.

Jesus had healed people who were ill and had been kind to the poor. Blind people could see, deaf people could hear, and lame people could walk because Jesus had healed them. Most important of all, Jesus had told people how much God loved them.

So as Jesus rode toward Jerusalem, a large crowd gathered. Soon the colt was walking over their soft cloaks instead of on the hard, stony ground. Then the colt felt cool palms under his hooves as people cut branches from the trees and laid them on the road.

All around them, people were shouting and cheering about Jesus, "Hosanna! Hosanna!"

The colt carried Jesus into the great city of Jerusalem. Jesus, the Lord and Savior of us all, had come!

Where these stories can be found in the Bible:

Creatures Great and Small, Genesis 1
Lots of Birds and Beasties, Genesis 6:10–8:5
A Raven, a Dove, and a Rainbow, Genesis 8:6–22
The Patient Camels, Genesis 37:3–28
Beasties in Egypt, Exodus 3:7–10; 7:14–12:32
The Donkey That Saw an Angel, Numbers 22:21–27
Balaam's Talking Donkey, Numbers 22:28–33
The Donkeys That Wandered, 1 Samuel 9:1–10:1
The Helpful Ravens, 1 Kings 17:1–6
A Big Fish and a Stormy Sea, Jonah 1:1–16
The Fish That Swallowed a Man, Jonah 1:17–2:10
The Tight-Mouthed Lions, Daniel 6:1–27
A Baby in the Cattle Shed, Luke 2:4–7
The Sheep That Heard Angels, Luke 2:8–16
The Camels That Followed a Star, Matthew 2:1–2
Camels, Gifts, and a King, Matthew 2:3–11
The Little Sparrows, Matthew 10:29–31
The Very Special Sheep, Luke 15:3–4; John 10:14–16
A Lost Sheep Is Found, Luke 15:5–7
The Colt That Carried a King, Luke 19:29–38